Shin pads

THE YOUNG SOCCER PLAYER

GARY LINEKER

D0339768

Soccer shoe

Goaltending strip

Dribbling with the inside of your foot

Screening the ball from your opponent

Dribbling with the outside of your foot

Stoddart

A DORLING KINDERSLEY BOOK

Editor Claire Bampton   **Art editor** Rebecca Johns

Project editor Louise Pritchard

Production Catherine Semark

Photographer John Garrett

Deputy editorial director Sophie Mitchell
Deputy art editor Miranda Kennedy

The young soccer players
Ben Blyth, Rene Brade, Scott Brealey, Alex Brennan, Ben Brennan,
Johnathan Crane, Tom Dove, Hannah Gardiner, Delroy Gill,
Adam Habtesellasse, Daniel Platel, Jamie Ross-Hulme, Angel Watson

First published in Canada in 1994 by
Stoddart Publishing Co. Limited
34 Lesmill Road, Toronto, Canada M3B 2T6

First published in Great Britain in 1994 by
Dorling Kindersley Limited,
9 Henrietta Street, London WC2E 8PS

Canadian Cataloguing in Publication Data

Lineker, Gary
The young soccer player

ISBN 0-7737-5655-8
1. Soccer for children – Juvenile literature.
I. Title.
GV944.2.L55 1994   J796.334'62   C94-930288-0

Color reproduction by Colourscan, Singapore
Printed by Graphicom in Italy

Contents

Use a slide tackle to clear the ball away from your opponent rather than to win possession.

Use your arm and elbow to cushion your fall.

To all young players

"SOCCER IS a wonderful game and I am fortunate to have been involved at the top level. I have so many memories to treasure – the excitement of playing with English teams Everton and Tottenham Hotspur, and the challenge of playing abroad for Spain's Barcelona, and more recently with Japan's Grampus Eight. One thing that I have learned is that you only get out of soccer what you put in. Probably the most important advice I can give you is to play fair and enjoy yourself. I hope very much that you have fun reading this book, and get as much enjoyment from soccer as I do. Good luck!"

Linesmen patrol the field to assist the referee. They use flags to indicate when a player fouls or when the ball goes out of play.

There are two linesmen. They each watch one half of the field.

Here the linesman is holding his flag out horizontally and pointing it across the field. He is indicating that one of the players is in an offside position.

A professional, adult match is played in two halves of 45 minutes each. The referee keeps note of any time lost for injuries or stoppages and adds it on to each half of the match.

The referee uses his whistle to indicate the start and end of each half of the match, and to draw attention to fouls.

A player will be given the red card and sent off the field for a serious offense.

A player can be shown the yellow card for bad fouls and persistent rule-breaking.

Rules of the game

SOCCER IS A GAME in which two sides of eleven players compete to put the ball into the opposing team's goal. There are rules to make the game run smoothly, enforced by the referee. Learn them when you start playing soccer so that they become second nature to you.

The field
A soccer field is oblong in shape and can be between 295 ft and 394 ft long, and 148 ft and 295 ft wide.

Goal line

Goal

Goal area

Halfway line

Center circle

Corner circle

Penalty arc

Penalty area

Touchline

Penalty spot

At kick-off, players must stand in their own half of the field, outside the center circle.

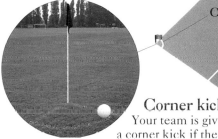

Corner kick
Your team is given a corner kick if the opposition kicks the ball over their own goal line. The opposition must stand more than 29.5 ft away from the corner circle.

Penalty kick
If a member of your team is fouled in your opponents' penalty area, your team will be awarded a penalty kick. The goaltender must stand on the goal line and all the other players must stand outside the penalty area and arc – until the kick has been taken.

A penalty kick is taken from the penalty spot.

After a goal is scored, the non-scoring side kicks off.

Touchline

In play
This ball is in play because it is not completely over the touchline.

Out of play
This ball is out of play because it has crossed the touchline completely.

Offside position
The offside rule is devised to prevent players from loitering around the opposition's goal area, waiting for an opportunity to score. You are offside if you are in your opponents' half of the field and closer to your opponents' goal than the ball, at the moment the ball was last touched. There are exceptions to this rule. You are not offside if an opponent touched the ball last, if there are two or more opponents between yourself and the goal line, or if you receive the ball directly from a throw-in, goal kick, corner kick, or drop ball.

Free kicks
You are awarded a free kick if you are fouled by the opposition. A free kick can be direct (from which you can score), or indirect (from which you cannot directly score). To signal for an indirect free kick, the referee holds his left arm in the air. Direct free kicks are usually awarded for more serious offenses.

What you need

WHEN BUYING A SOCCER kit, there are four points you should keep in mind. Each piece should be comfortable, durable, lightweight, and an aid to your performance. The most important item is your shoes. You should choose a pair that support your feet firmly, especially around your ankles. To see whether they fit comfortably, wear soccer socks when trying them on in the store. Never buy shoes a size too big thinking you will grow into them. If you do, you will find it hard to get any sense of touch for the ball, and you may also get painful blisters.

Long-sleeved shirts are generally worn in the winter. Short-sleeved shirts may be worn in the summer if preferred.

Soccer shoes

Shoes are designed to help you use both the inside and outside of your foot. Make sure that the shoes are flexible. Choose shoes made of good-quality leather. The softer the leather, the easier it is to feel the ball.

A wide tongue under the laces will make the shoe more comfortable.

Interchangeable studs

"Astro" boot with molded studs

Studs

Screw-in studs let you adapt your shoe to make it suitable for all conditions. You will also need a stud wrench in order to ensure that the studs are secured firmly.

Flat rubber studs for hard grounds

Aluminum studs for wet and slippery conditions

Nylon studs for a field that is soft, yet firm

"Astro boot"

This is really a training shoe adapted for use on artificial grass. A pattern of tiny molded studs provides a near-perfect grip. This shoe has 73 more studs than a normal soccer shoe.

You can keep your socks up with garters or a narrow length of bandage.

Shin pads

Lightweight shin pads provide protection for a very vulnerable and sensitive part of your body. By guarding against bruises and cuts, shin pads will boost your confidence when going into a tackle.

Shin pads can be taped or tied around your legs.

Wear shin pads when you practice, as well as for matches.

What to wear on the field

When choosing clothing, the material is an important consideration. Cotton is still the most popular and practical because unlike synthetic materials, it absorbs sweat. Shorts should be loose enough to allow you freedom of movement, while shirts should be comfortable, neither too tight nor too loose.

Balls

Soccer balls used for matches must be made of an approved material, such as leather. Plastic balls can provide fun on the beach or in the yard. However, if you wish to improve your feel for the ball, it is best to practice with one as similar as possible to the real thing.

Goaltending gloves

Although gloves are a vital aid in handling, they must not be allowed to restrict the movement of your fingers and thumbs. So before buying, always check for both comfort and flexibility.

Dampen the palms of your gloves before a match to make them less slippery.

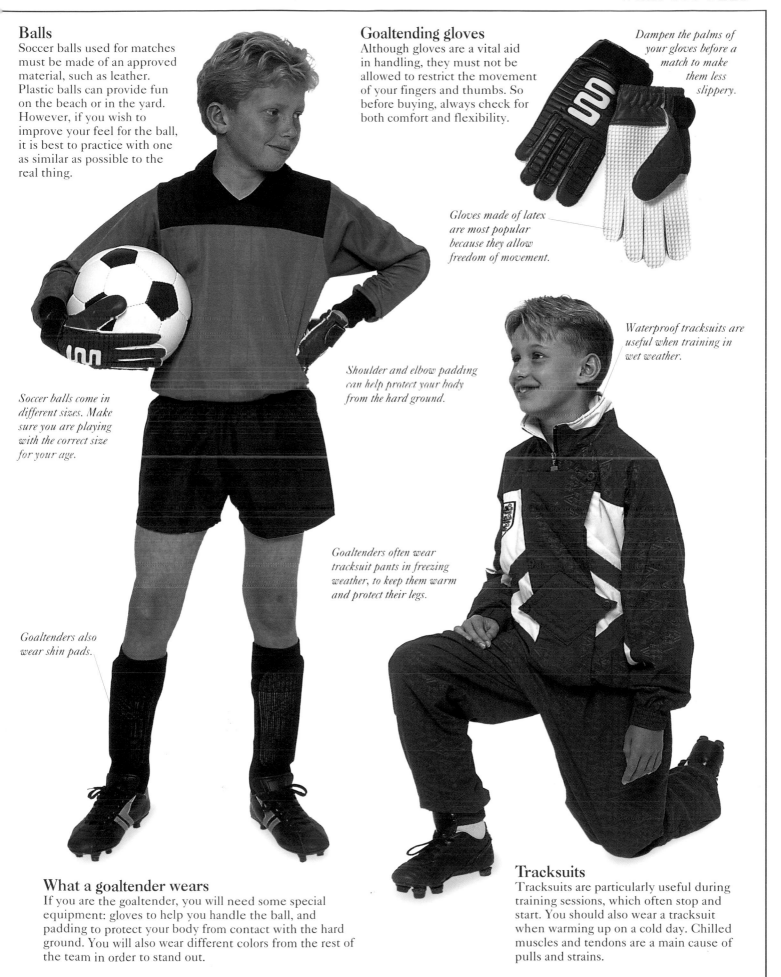

Gloves made of latex are most popular because they allow freedom of movement.

Shoulder and elbow padding can help protect your body from the hard ground.

Waterproof tracksuits are useful when training in wet weather.

Soccer balls come in different sizes. Make sure you are playing with the correct size for your age.

Goaltenders often wear tracksuit pants in freezing weather, to keep them warm and protect their legs.

Goaltenders also wear shin pads.

What a goaltender wears

If you are the goaltender, you will need some special equipment: gloves to help you handle the ball, and padding to protect your body from contact with the hard ground. You will also wear different colors from the rest of the team in order to stand out.

Tracksuits

Tracksuits are particularly useful during training sessions, which often stop and start. You should also wear a tracksuit when warming up on a cold day. Chilled muscles and tendons are a main cause of pulls and strains.

Basic passing

SOCCER IS A TEAM GAME, so essentially it involves passing the ball between teammates. Without passing, soccer would simply be a game played by eleven individuals. There are several different types of passes and you must select the one you use to suit each situation. Always pass the ball so that your teammate can control it, and avoid losing possession. Passing the ball gives you an opportunity to move into space, perhaps to pick up a return pass.

3 Position yourself over the ball and strike it in the middle. This will keep the ball low. Direct your follow-through toward your target. The ball will travel in whatever direction your foot is facing.

Use your arms to balance your body.

Your follow-through controls the speed of the ball and also, to some extent, the accuracy of the pass.

Push pass

1 The push pass is the most accurate way to get the ball to a nearby teammate, because a large area of your shoe comes into contact with the ball. Place your non-kicking foot near the ball.

2 Keeping your eyes on the ball, turn your kicking leg out from your hip. Your foot should be at right angles to your target. Aim to kick the ball with the inside of your foot.

"That vital first touch tells you everything about ... a man."
Joe Mercer, former England manager

Backheel pass

1 You will normally use the backheel pass as a surprise move to avoid a tackle. The nature of the pass makes it impossible for you to see your target, so don't use it too often, and never if you are close to your own goal. Place your supporting foot close to the ball. Lower your head and try to watch the ball as you kick it. Hit the ball with the back of your heel, using a short, sharp action, little more than a tap.

Watch the ball closely to minimize the risk of miskicking.

2 Because backheel passes are usually short-range, you do not need to follow through. Keep your body balanced so you are ready to move away as soon as you have completed the pass.

Keep your kicking foot in a horizontal position so that your heel forms a solid base.

Strike through the center of the ball.

Perform the pass as quickly as possible, before your opponents realize what is happening.

Pass directed into the path of a teammate

1 If your teammate is running past an opponent into space, you can pass the ball and avoid the danger of an interception. You need to anticipate just where your teammate will be in a few seconds time, and then pass the ball accordingly. Use whichever pass is most suitable for the situation.

Your teammate will run past an opponent into space.

2 Try to pass the ball straight into your teammate's path. Your teammate should be able to run up to the ball and not have to change speed or direction. You must be careful to time the pass so that your teammate is not caught offside.

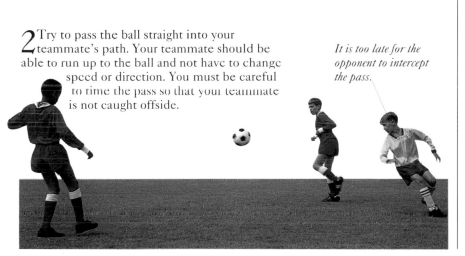

It is too late for the opponent to intercept the pass.

Lofted pass

Use the lofted pass to get the ball to a teammate farther up the field. Approach the ball at an angle to increase your power potential. Lean back and look up to make sure you are aiming toward your targeted teammate. Lift your kicking leg into a high backswing and turn your body into the ball. Keeping your ankle firm, kick the bottom of the ball with your instep. The ball's flight should be high enough to avoid your opponents' reach.

Look toward your targeted teammate.

Push the ball a bit in front of you so that you can take a long run up to it.

Wall pass

1 The wall pass, also known as the "one-two," is a simple way for two attackers to overcome a single defender by passing the ball quickly from one to the other. Run with the ball until you are a few yards away from the defender. Look up to see where your teammate is positioned. Using a push pass, kick the ball wide to your teammate, past the defender.

Anticipate the position of your teammate.

Your teammate will pick up the ball and pass it back quickly.

2 When you have passed the ball, continue running forward into space and be ready to pick up the return ball. The defender cannot follow you without leaving your teammate unopposed, in possession of the ball.

Your guard will remain with you.

3 Your teammate should return the ball to you immediately. Pick up the ball quickly, control it, and run on toward the goal before the defender has a chance to intercept. Your teammate has acted as a wall, "bouncing" the ball back to you.

Kicking skills

THERE ARE MANY different ways to direct a soccer ball. You can use the full instep of your foot, the inside or outside of your foot, your toe, or your heel. You can swerve the ball, push it, or chip it, and by altering the position of your head and supporting foot, you can loft the ball or keep it low. After you have learned the basic passing skills, gradually master all the different kicking skills. Only then will you be able to assess a situation properly and decide which kick is most appropriate. It is also important for you to learn how to kick the ball with both your left and your right foot.

To lift the ball, lean slightly backward as you kick.

Swerving the ball with the inside of the foot

To swerve the ball around your opponent, kick the ball slightly left of center with the inside of your left foot (or slightly right of center with the inside of your right foot). The ball will swerve from left to right (or right to left) in an arc.

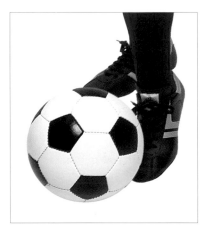

Inside story

In this picture I am kicking the ball with the inside of my foot. Notice that at the moment of impact my body is balanced. I am leaning slightly backward, allowing my leg to swing forward and lift the ball slightly.

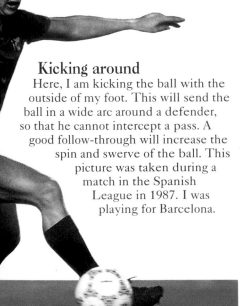

Kicking around

Here, I am kicking the ball with the outside of my foot. This will send the ball in a wide arc around a defender, so that he cannot intercept a pass. A good follow-through will increase the spin and swerve of the ball. This picture was taken during a match in the Spanish League in 1987. I was playing for Barcelona.

Swerving the ball with the outside of the foot

Another way to swerve the ball is to kick it slightly left of center with the outside of your right foot (or slightly right of center with the outside of your left foot). As you kick, let your foot slide along the ball, causing it to spin from left to right (or right to left).

Long-range kick

1 It is important for you to learn how to kick the ball a long way so that you can make contact with teammates farther up the field. Push the ball slightly ahead of you so that you can take a running start. Don't allow your supporting foot to get too close to the ball.

Spread your arms outward and backward to help you balance.

2 Lift your kicking leg into a high backswing as you turn your body into the ball.

3 Kick the lower area of the ball with your instep. To follow through, trace the flight of the ball with your active foot.

Lean backward as you kick the ball to lift it and make it travel a long distance.

Volleying the ball

A volley is a pass made by kicking the ball while it is still in the air. It is essentially a stabbing action with very little follow-through. First, keep your eyes focused firmly on the approaching ball. Then place your knee and head over the ball, swing back your leg, and kick it with the full instep of your foot. This will keep the ball low. Note the angle and balance of my body. This has enabled me to put my full power behind the ball.

Keep your ankle firm on impact. This will give power to your volley.

Weighted cross

Here, I have just used a weighted cross to pass the ball accurately to a teammate. The weight, or strength, of this pass depends largely on the length of your backswing and the position of your body. If you lean back and increase your backswing, the ball will travel quite a long way.

Chipping the ball

If the goaltender comes off the goal line, you can chip the ball into the goal. Put the end of your toe under the ball and angle your foot downward. Lean backward and kick the ball with a stabbing action. The ball will rise steeply over the goaltender's head and spin backward, making it slow down and fall into the goal. There is no need for a follow-through.

You can also use a chip to get the ball past a defender, while you run past and pick it up again.

Place your supporting foot as close to the side of the ball as possible.

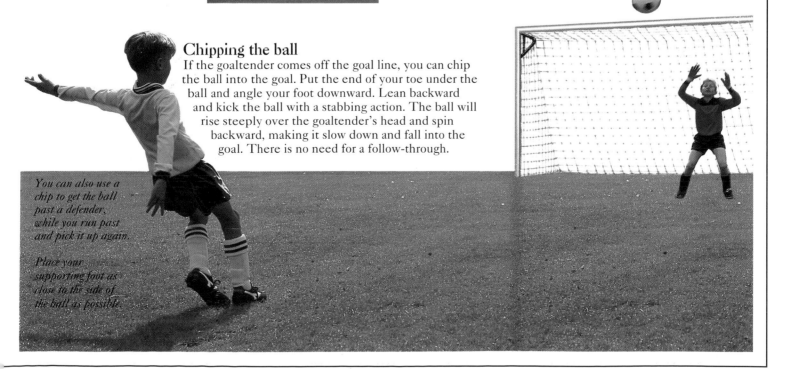

Ball control

M ASTERY OF THE BALL is the key to soccer success. Whether you control the ball using your foot, thigh, chest, or head, depends on the height at which it reaches you. The ball usually arrives at speed so you must learn to cushion and absorb the force of it. When you begin to play soccer, practice ball control standing still. Remember, though, you won't be given the time to do this in a match. So, as soon as possible, you must learn to get to the ball quickly, control it, and move off, all in the same flowing movement.

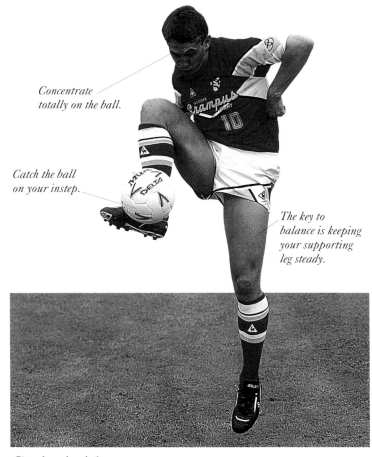

Concentrate totally on the ball.

Catch the ball on your instep.

The key to balance is keeping your supporting leg steady.

Trapping with the sole of the foot

When it is necessary to trap the ball dead, you should trap it between the sole of your foot and the ground. As the ball approaches, lift your foot with your toes pointing upward and allow the ball to wedge itself under your shoe. Try to develop a soft touch.

Getting it right

Here, I am taming a volley with the inside of my foot. You will notice that I am balanced on the toes of one foot and yet still look solid and secure. This picture was taken during my debut for Grampus Eight in Japan.

Taming a volley with the inside of the foot

When receiving a ball in this way, good balance is essential because you may have to raise your foot quite high. Make sure you move your foot backward to absorb the impact. Think of this movement as a follow-through in reverse; the longer your foot stays in contact with the ball, the more control you will have.

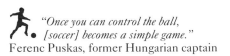
"Once you can control the ball, [soccer] becomes a simple game."
Ferenc Puskas, former Hungarian captain

Controlling on the thigh

When the ball comes to you at an awkward height – too high to control with your foot, yet too low for your chest – your thigh can be invaluable. If you lean slightly backward to receive the ball, you will be able to balance yourself with your arms.

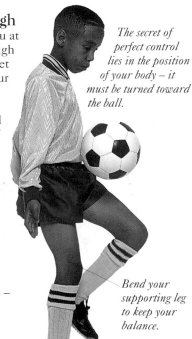

The secret of perfect control lies in the position of your body – it must be turned toward the ball.

Giving yourself time
Good control gains you time – time to look around and time to decide on your next move.

Bend your supporting leg to keep your balance.

Controlling on the chest

1 Your chest is a strong and wide area on which to cushion a ball, but it also happens to be quite hard. To prepare yourself for the impact of the ball, square your body toward its flight. At the same time extend your arms. This will help you balance and avoid any immediate danger of the ball hitting your hands or arms.

Keep your head centered over your shoulders to ensure a well-balanced body.

Keep your arms away from your body and meet the ball with your chest pushed out.

Relax your chest as you control the ball.

Either bend or straighten your knees to achieve the right height for good chest contact.

2 As you receive the ball, arch your back and puff out your chest. Balls at this height are often traveling quickly, but don't tense your muscles. If you do, the ball will simply bounce away. Your upper body will need to sway back to absorb the impact.

Loosen your wrists – this will help relax the rest of your body.

3 As you bring the ball down to your feet, move your shoulders forward so that the ball drops straight down. Make sure your knees are bent and your feet are placed wide apart to provide a solid base.

Screening the ball

When you have no immediate teammate to pass to, you should protect the ball by screening it. To do this, put your body between the opponent and the ball. Although this is a perfectly legitimate tactic, you must be careful not to use your arms to hold off the would-be tackler.

Keeping possession

This is a picture of me screening the ball from my opponent. As you can see, I am leaning over the ball, just about to make my next move. This was a pre-season game in July 1989 between my team, Tottenham Hotspur FC, and the Bohemians in Dublin, Ireland.

"The secret of [soccer] is to do the simple things supremely well." Bobby Moore, former England captain

The first touch
When controlling the ball, your first touch is very important.

While your body shields the ball, you should be thinking about your next move.

Keep the ball as far away from the opponent as possible.

Heading

D URING A MATCH, the ball can spend as much time in the air as it does on the ground, so heading is a skill that you must master. Even goaltenders occasionally need to head the ball. Heading is one of the most exciting features of a match. To be a great header of the ball you must be athletic, fearless, and skillful. It is a difficult technique to master because it requires both good positioning and excellent timing. The great secret of heading is to attack the ball and not let the ball attack you!

As you move forward, tense your neck muscles so that your head stays firm.

Basic header
Create a solid base with your feet and relax your body. Keep your eyes on the ball to receive it with accuracy. Pull your head and body back, then push yourself forward with force. Meet the ball with the middle of your forehead and aim it toward your targeted area.

Keep your feet apart to improve your balance and control.

Defensive header
To clear the ball away from the goal mouth, it must go as far and as high as possible. Run into your jump and push off from one foot. Meet the ball at the top of your jump, using your forehead.

Diving header
You need to be courageous to perform a diving header because you will normally use it to meet a low ball in a crowded goal area. Dive forward into a horizontal position, throw your arms out in front of you. This will add strength to your dive and help cushion your fall.

Firmly hit the top half of the ball with the middle of your forehead. This will keep the ball down.

Keep your eyes focused on the ball as you dive.

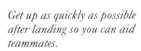

Get up as quickly as possible after landing so you can aid teammates.

Timing of the header

Perfect timing for a header is vital if there are two players going for the ball at once. It is something that you will only learn from practice. Push off from one foot to gain extra height. Meet the ball at the highest point of your jump, while your opponent is already on the way down or still rising.

🏃 *Remember not to use your arms to push your opponent out of the way. If you do, you will give away a free kick.*

🏃 *"Make the ball your friend."* Pelé, the legendary Brazilian striker

Perfect timing

I'm not really smiling, although perhaps I should be! I've just outjumped my opponent by simply taking off a second earlier. I've met the ball at the top of my jump with the middle of my forehead. For this header, at least, my timing was perfect.

The ball should travel with force in a straight line toward your target.

Diving in

Having found space just outside the goal area, I have just performed an unopposed diving header. Due to a lack of attention from my opponents, I had time to control the ball and steer it toward the goal mouth. In this position my arms will cushion my fall and help me get back on to my feet as quickly as possible.

Playing to win

With my opponent close behind, this is very much anyone's ball. Nottingham Forest's Steve Hodge and I are both poised, ready to head the ball. My neck muscles are clenched and my eyes are firmly focused on the ball. I have jumped off the ground from one foot, and am in the process of thrusting my body forward to head the ball.

Do not wait for the ball to reach you – move forward to meet it yourself.

Dribbling

THE ULTIMATE SKILL of close control is dribbling. This involves running with the ball close to your feet, and pushing it forward with quick, sharp kicks. When you dribble, the ball must look as though it is tied to your shoelaces. A good dribbler who is prepared to take the ball through a crowded goal area can cause chaos among the defense. But dribbling has its risks, and all too often players lose possession when they are over-ambitious. Learn to ration your runs. Soccer is still essentially a passing game.

Dribbling practice
Place a row of plastic cones in a straight line about six feet apart, and practice dribbling around them. The position of the cones will force you to use both sides of your foot.

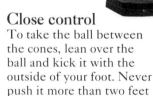

Basic dribbling
To dribble in a straight line, alternately use both the inside and outside of your foot. This gives you the opportunity to change direction quickly and with precision. Kick the ball using gentle, yet sharp taps. Keep the ball far enough in front of you so that you can see both it and the other players around you. Remain in control of the ball at all times.

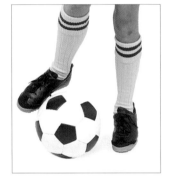

Push the ball a short distance in front of you with the instep of your foot.

Straighten up the ball with the outside of the same foot. Repeat this sequence to form a rhythm.

Close control
To take the ball between the cones, lean over the ball and kick it with the outside of your foot. Never push it more than two feet away from your foot.

Getting past an opponent

1 If you decide to take on an opponent rather than pass the ball to a teammate, you can pretend to go one way before going another. As you approach, make sure that the ball stays close to your foot so that you do not give your opponent the opportunity to make a successful tackle.

2 Your opponent will probably take up a diagonal tackling position. This will force you to move in a certain direction.

3 Push the ball forward with the inside of your foot without losing control. Your opponent will begin to cover your move by stepping toward the ball.

Changing direction
To move around the cone, transfer the ball to the inside of your foot and push it a short way forward.

Use your arms to help you balance.

Running with the ball
This type of dribbling will only work if you have a lot of space in front of you and the ability to run fast. Run flat out, pushing the ball well ahead so that you do not have to check your stride. Gradually reduce the number of kicks and look up to decide on your next move. Because my strides are so large here, I need to maintain perfect control and balance.

Dribble to win
Never dribble in your own goal area and never dribble past an opponent if a simple wall pass will achieve the same result.

"Knowing when to dribble, when to pass – this is the true skill." *Roberto Baggio, of the Italian team*

"Learn to dribble and to think, all at the same time." *Geoff Hurst, England's hat-trick hero of the 1966 World Cup*

Keep the ball as close as possible to your foot.

Gathering speed
As you practice dribbling, you will speed up. Time yourself to see how fast you can dribble without losing control.

4 When your opponent moves one way, quickly lean and push the ball in the opposite direction with the outside of your foot. You need to be quick and agile to outwit your opponent.

Dribbling the ball invites challenges. Always wear shin pads.

Never let the ball move more than two feet away from your foot.

Tackling

ALL SOCCER PLAYERS need to learn the skill of tackling. The aims of a tackle are to make your opponent lose possession of the ball and to gain possession yourself. There are two basic positions you can use when going in for a tackle: the frontal position, in which you face your opponent square on, and the diagonal position, in which you put yourself to one side of your opponent. Timing, positional sense, and the ability to read the game are all important, but only practice will improve your skills.

Keep your eyes on the ball.

Bend your knees to help you balance and strengthen your tackle.

Block tackle

You will normally use the block tackle when both you and your opponent have an equal chance of winning the ball. You can approach your opponent from either a frontal or a diagonal position. Putting your full weight behind the tackle, place the inside of your foot against the center of the ball, just as your opponent is about to pass it. If the ball becomes stuck between your opponent's feet and your own, try to flick it away.

In focus
When tackling, watch the ball, not your opponent.

Slide tackle

1 Use a slide tackle to clear the ball away from your opponent rather than to win possession. The timing of this tackle should be extremely accurate, so do not be tempted to move in too soon. Try to time your tackle so that you can slide the ball away just before your opponent attempts a pass. Run toward your opponent and the ball.

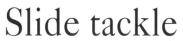

Timing it right
Knowing *when* to tackle is just as important as knowing *how* to tackle.

2 Bend your supporting leg to prepare yourself for the slide. Be careful not to kick or trip up your opponent, or you will give away a free kick.

Resist the temptation to slide in too soon.

Intercepting a pass

1 You should be able to win the ball without any physical contact simply by intercepting the ball. Try to intercept the ball as your opponent passes it to a teammate. Judge the speed of the pass, and move quickly along the shortest route to the line of the ball.

Do not give your opponent time to control the ball.

Judge the speed of the ball and the position at which you will be able to intercept it.

Your teammate should be ready to pick up a pass.

2 When you intercept the pass, bring the moving ball under control with the inside of your foot. Turn your back to your opponent and pass the ball to a teammate as soon as possible, before your opponent tries to tackle you and regain control.

Your opponent will try to run off with the ball. Wrap your leg firmly around the ball to avoid this situation.

3 Using your instep, try to hook or push the ball as far away as possible. Slide down low in front of your opponent and scoop your leg around the ball. Use the full weight of your body to help you win the ball.

Use your arm and elbow to cushion your fall.

Slide time
This picture clearly shows a situation where my opponent has failed to tackle me successfully. He has made a perfectly fair challenge, surprising me and taking the ball from my foot. Unfortunately for him, he has not cleared the ball wide enough, and I am able to jump over his leg, pick up the ball, and carry on. He has left me with the ball while putting himself temporarily out of action.

The dead ball

W HEN THE BALL goes off the field, or the referee stops the match, the ball must be brought back into play. It is most important that you learn the appropriate rules, and use each "dead ball" situation to your full advantage. It is a good idea for your team to have a variety of pre-planned moves for when corners, free kicks, and throw-ins are taken. Practice such moves so that during matches they are second nature to you.

Spread your fingers wide around the ball.

Hold the ball above your head as you run, then take it farther back just before you throw.

2 Take the ball back behind your head as far as you can. Arch your back and bend your leading leg.

Long throw-in

1 If the opposing team kicks the ball over the touchline, you will be awarded a throw-in. Take the throw from the point where the ball crossed the line. The ball must be thrown from behind your head with both hands. Run up to the touchline just before you throw; this will give you power to throw the ball a long way.

The penalty spot is 36 ft from the center of the goal line.

An opponent must stand more than 29.5 ft away from the ball.

Penalty kick

Because your team will expect you to score a goal, taking a penalty kick can be extremely nerve-wracking. Before you take the shot, choose which side of the goal you are going to aim for without giving the goaltender any idea of your intentions. Low shots are normally the most difficult to save. In this picture I have chosen my targeted area and am simply concentrating on hitting the ball, low and hard, just inside the goaltender's right-hand post.

Corner kick

Take the corner kick from the corner circle on the side of the field where the ball went over the goal line. You can score directly from a corner. Kick the ball so that it swerves toward either the near or far posts – one of the hardest areas to defend – or follow your team's pre-planned tactic.

3 Bring your weight onto your leading leg and whip your body forward as you throw the ball. Bend your body from your waist using your whole body to add power to the throw – your back and shoulders as well as your arms.

The follow-through will help you reach your desired target.

Throw the ball so that your targeted teammate will not have to check his stride.

4 As you release the ball, use your arms and fingers to guide it in the right direction. After you have completed the throw, remember to get right back into the action of the match.

Make sure that your front foot is on or behind the touchline.

Quick throw-in

1 You can surprise the opposition by taking a quick throw-in. It is advisable for the player nearest to the ball to take the throw-in. Stand on or behind the touchline.

2 Even though you need to throw the ball as quickly as possible, you must remember to take the ball back behind your head and hold it with both hands.

3 Throw the ball so that a teammate can gain instant control. If all your teammates are being guarded, throw the ball to a player who can pass it back to you as soon as you run onto the field again.

Free kick

When awarded a free kick, a penalty, or a corner, you must wait for the referee's signal before you kick the ball.

Take the free kick from where the offense occured. When you take a direct free kick in front of the goal, your opposition will set up a wall of players to block your vision of the goal. If you want to shoot, you will either have to swerve the ball around the wall or chip it over the top. Alternatively, you could pass the ball to an unguarded teammate.

No opponent is allowed within 29.5 ft of the ball.

21

Shooting

TO WIN A MATCH you must score more goals than the
opposing team. Goals can be scored from brilliantly planned
shots or just from spotting a good opportunity. There are
numerous ways to shoot the ball into the goal. You can shoot
from the ground or volley the ball. You can use an
overhead kick or a header. If you want to be a good
striker, you should master all of the shooting techniques.
Aim to be so familiar with the goal that you do not have
to look at it before making your shot, and shoot at
every scoring opportunity. Remember – you might not
score each time you shoot, but you will never score
unless you shoot.

*Keep your head down
over the ball, to keep
the shot low.*

*Bring the knee of
your kicking leg over
the ball to keep the
shot low.*

Shooting from the ground
This is one of the most common ways for
you to shoot. First, put your supporting
foot close to the ball and point it toward
the target. Take a small backswing with
your kicking leg, then, with your toes
pointing down, kick the ball hard with
your instep.

Volleying

1 If the ball approaches you at a high
level you can use a volley to shoot. This
involves shooting as you bring the ball
under control. First, make sure you are in
a position to receive the ball comfortably.
Spread your arms wide to help you
balance. I like to use this shot
because it has two advantages:
it often comes as a surprise to
my opponents and it creates
a great deal of power.

*You should know where
the goal is without
having to look.*

Keep your eyes on the ball.

2 Lean away from the
approaching ball to keep
it low when you shoot. Bring
your head and your knee over
the ball. As the instep of your
kicking foot comes in contact with
the ball in the air, bring the ball with
you and aim it in the direction of the
goal. I use the whole of my body weight
to kick the ball. This usually makes it a
very accurate shot.

Sliding in a ground shot

If a defender is trying to clear the ball away from a crowded goal, you may be able to find an opportunity to slide in a ground shot. Run up toward the ball and begin to slide in on your leg nearest to the defender. Slide to one side of the defender and stretch your leg forward with all your strength. Use your arm for support. Kick the ball into the goal with a scooping action. You must not make contact with your opponent's foot before touching the ball.

The slide shot will often come as a surprise to your opponents.

Always think one step ahead of a situation. If you have a chance to shoot – take it.

Sliding shots work better on a wet field.

3 There is no follow-through after a volley. When the ball leaves your foot, quickly run toward the goal. I always follow up my shot, just in case the ball rebounds off the goaltender and gives me a chance to shoot again.

You are now facing the goal and able to run forward.

Opportunist goal

Here I have seen an opportunity, taken it, and scored. Under heavy pressure from two defenders, I used a sliding shot to knock the ball out of their control and into the goal.

Overhead kick

If I have my back to the opposition's goal I sometimes use the overhead kick to shoot. In this picture I have taken off from my non-kicking foot and arched the top half of my body backward. My kicking leg has automatically swung up as my non-kicking leg swung down. I have kicked the ball with the front of my foot, and am now preparing to cushion the fall with my arms.

Basic goaltending

G OALTENDERS PROBABLY have one of the most demanding roles in soccer. When in goal you need to be brave, athletic, calm, and above all, intelligent. The penalty area is your domain and you decide how challenges to it are answered. Once you have the ball safely in your hands, you will be ready to launch the next counterattack with a goal kick or a quick throw. Goaltenders do much more than just stop shots.

Your arms work in counterbalance – as your throwing arm rises, your other arm falls.

Overarm throw

1 The overarm throw is for distance and you will usually use it when the opposition has swarmed forward to attack. You should throw the ball before their defense has a chance to move back into position. While keeping your arm straight, take the ball back and point your non-throwing arm and leading foot toward the target.

Use the length of your body to stretch, taking the ball as far back as possible.

2 Keeping your throwing arm rigid, turn your hips toward your target. The longer the arc of your arm, the longer the throw. The speed of your arm will also determine distance.

3 Once you are in the correct position, throw the ball high enough to clear opposing players, but still low enough for your teammate to be able to control instantly.

As you let go of the ball, flick your wrist.

Underarm throw

1 The underarm throw is for short-range passes and you will normally use it as a safety measure to ensure that you do not give away possession of the ball. Point your leading foot in the direction of your target.

Don't forget
• You are not allowed to pick up a back pass from a defender.

For the moment, your eyes should concentrate on the targeted defender.

2 Bring the ball into play by taking a step forward and bending your back leg. Your head should remain still throughout the movement.

Keep your other arm close to your body for a more streamlined shape.

Gathering a ground shot

1 To gather a ground shot, keep your body behind the ball, bend down on one knee, and be prepared for the awkward last-second bounce. Tilt your body slightly forward, so that if you mishandle, it will be much easier for you to dive on the ball.

2 Scoop the ball safely into your chest as quickly as possible. Note that your knee has formed its own barrier.

3 Cup the palms of both of your hands around the ball to prevent it from spilling out. Now it belongs to you. Spread your fingers so that your little fingers nearly touch. Keep your head steady and your upper body folded over the ball.

Position of hands

Spread your fingers and thumbs to the side and behind the ball to form a W-shape. The space between each hand should be as small as possible. Bend your forearms slightly and use them as shock absorbers to take the speed off the ball.

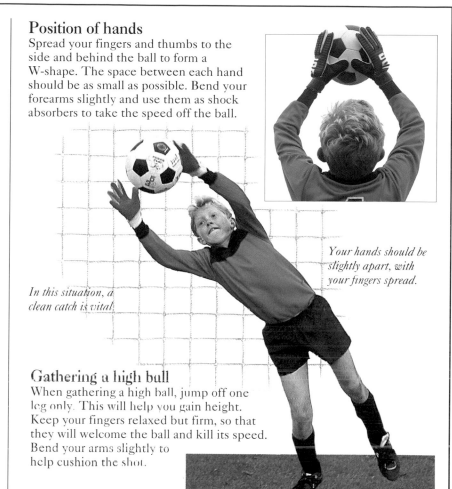

Your hands should be slightly apart, with your fingers spread.

In this situation, a clean catch is vital.

Gathering a high ball

When gathering a high ball, jump off one leg only. This will help you gain height. Keep your fingers relaxed but firm, so that they will welcome the ball and kill its speed. Bend your arms slightly to help cushion the shot.

3 As you bring your arm forward to throw the ball, you are close to the point of no return. If there is any danger of an interception, now is the moment to check and keep possession. So stay alert and be very much aware of the changing situation around you.

Take a last-second look at the situation.

Bend your back leg to ensure a low body position.

Keep your leading leg firm to aid a quick recovery.

4 Roll the ball low, ideally along the ground, keeping your arm straight. Aim slightly in front of your teammate. Remember to follow through. This ensures accuracy, while putting enough speed on the ball to minimize the danger of an interception.

Now prepare for the possibility of a return pass.

Your trailing leg provides the thrust.

Use your whole body in the follow-through, not just your arm.

Goaltending

I F YOU ARE a goaltender you will need to develop quick reactions, excellent concentration, and good handling skills. Unless you save goals, you can never hope to be described as a good goaltender. You will perform skills unique to goaltending, such as diving saves and punches to the ball, and use tactics that make it difficult for attackers to score. As well as saving the ball, you will also need to learn how to clear the ball from the goal area.

Diving save

Here I have had a clear run at the goal and have shot from just inside the box. The goaltender has been forced to dive across the goal to reach the ball. His arms are stretched and ready to bring the ball close to his body.

Saving a low shot

When an attacker shoots a low ball you must dive to save it. As the ball approaches, dive sideways to form a barrier, then fall on top of it. Not only will your body form a wall, but your legs will also form an obstruction. Pull the ball tightly to your body to avoid the risk of a rebound into the path of an opponent.

Hold the ball with one of your hands behind the ball and one of your hands on top.

Goaltender's punt

1 To bring the ball back into play, use either a goal kick (a long-range kick from the goal area), a drop kick, or a punt. A punt involves kicking the ball after it has been dropped from your hands. This allows the ball to travel over a great distance. A drop kick involves the same basic principles, but you should not strike the ball until it has hit the ground. To perform a drop kick or a punt, hold the ball out in front of your body. Bend your knees, and look to check where your teammates are on the field.

"For a goaltender, positioning is everything."
Lev Yashin, Russian goaltender

2 Drop the ball and watch it fall, keeping your head steady. Don't allow yourself to be distracted.

Total concentration on the ball is most important at this stage.

Hold the ball well away from your body.

3 Place your non-kicking foot behind the ball and tilt your body slightly forward. Straighten your kicking leg from the hip.

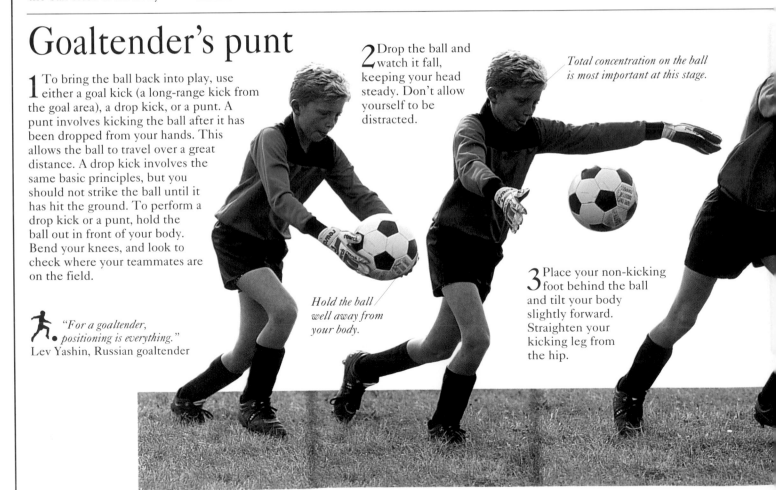

Narrowing the angle

1 If an attacker has broken free from the defense with the ball and you stay on your goal line, you will give your opponent a large area at which to shoot.

The goal looks very big to the attacker.

2 Move steadily away from your goal line toward the ball. This will reduce the area of the goal at which your opponent has to shoot. Your timing and positioning must be exact. If you come out too soon, your opponent can dribble around you and score; if you come out too far, your opponent may chip the ball over your head.

Punching the ball

When you punch the ball away you must aim for height and distance to give your teammates time to regroup. Clench your fists together and keep your wrists firm. As the ball comes toward you, punch the bottom half of the ball as hard and high as you can.

Saving the ball
Here Romanian goaltender Silviu Lung has punched the ball straight over my head to stop me from scoring. The match was a World Cup qualifier in 1985.

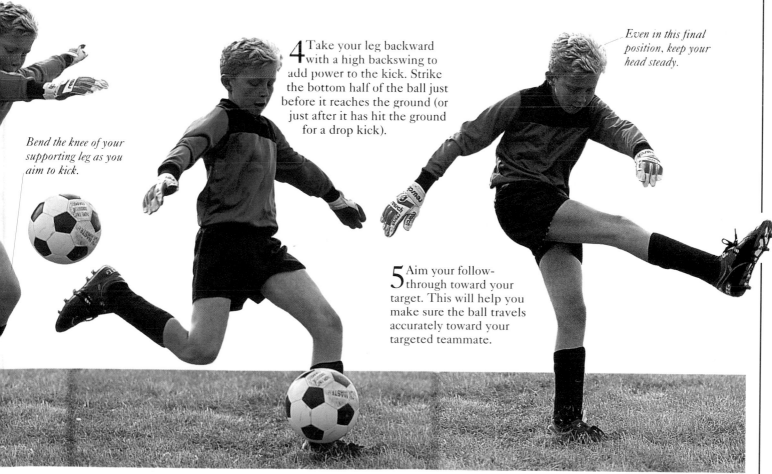

Bend the knee of your supporting leg as you aim to kick.

4 Take your leg backward with a high backswing to add power to the kick. Strike the bottom half of the ball just before it reaches the ground (or just after it has hit the ground for a drop kick).

Even in this final position, keep your head steady.

5 Aim your follow-through toward your target. This will help you make sure the ball travels accurately toward your targeted teammate.

On the attack

THE PLAYER people cheer is the one who scores the goal, but the supplier of the final pass often deserves just as much credit. The vast majority of goals come as a result of attacking tactics worked out before the match. Some of these are sequences of passes from a free kick, called "set pieces"; others are not so precisely planned and are just part of the flow of play. It is useful for your team to plan strategies that will break down the defenses of your opponents. There are different things you can try, but the tactics that you use must be suited to the particular talents of the players on your team. So practice first to find out what everyone can do best.

Crossing the ball

A cross into the goal area often results in a goal. If you are supplying a cross, make sure you aim it toward a particular teammate, ideally one that you know is good at heading the ball. It is important that you look up to see who is the best person to target before you cross the ball. It is a pity to waste a goal-scoring opportunity by providing a poor cross.

Assess the situation in front of the goal and cross the ball as soon as you can – before a defender has the chance to tackle you.

Drawing defenders wide

1 One of the best ways for an attacking team to create space is for some of them to "run off" the ball. This is when teammates confuse their opponents by running in a certain direction even if they are not about to receive the ball. It is sometimes difficult to find space to receive the ball in a crowded goal area. So if your team is attacking, some players can run wide, pretending they are going to receive the ball. These players will hopefully draw defenders with them, leaving a teammate "unmarked" or unguarded.

You must be careful to stay onside as you draw the defender wide.

The defender has to follow you in case you are running to receive the ball.

Another defender is drawn out wide the other way.

The player with the ball should look up to see who to pass to.

How to lose a guard

The defender has to try to watch you and the ball at the same time.

You can receive the ball unopposed.

1 The ability to get away from your guard is one of the skills you will need if you want to be a great goal scorer. When you want to receive a pass, make a run toward the teammate who has the ball. Your guard should follow you.

2 Just before your teammate passes the ball, confuse your guard by checking, or stopping quickly, then moving away in another direction. If you change direction quickly, your guard will be left behind.

3 Your teammate must pass the ball to you as soon you change direction. The defender will not have time to recover and intercept. Speed off the mark provides the final step in your team's attacking move.

2 Pass the ball to the attacker who is left in the space created. That player then has time to control the ball, turn, and shoot. The timing of the pass is often very important. If it is delayed too long there is a danger of both of the attackers being offside. If the ball is passed too early, the defenders may be able to get back to intercept.

To be onside the attackers must keep two defenders between them and the goal at the moment the ball is passed.

The central attacker has a perfect opportunity to score.

The player with the ball should pass with extreme accuracy.

On the defense

I F YOUR TEAM is defending, your goal is to prevent the other team from coming forward with the ball, and gain possession. Defenders must understand their role in a team's plan. There are two main systems of defense that you can use: "man-for-man guarding" where each defender guards a particular opponent, and "the zonal system" in which each defender has a particular area of the field to protect. But, as in all systems, you must be flexible.

Keep alert

I am known to be a striker, so goaltenders usually keep an eye on what I am doing during set pieces. They are then ready to try to block my shot or header. But my team can surprise them by crossing to someone else.

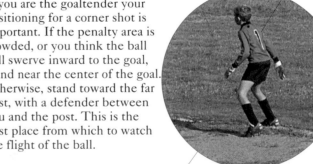

Defending against a corner

Defender and attacker

If you are defending while guarding the player most likely to receive the ball, position yourself between that person and the goal. Stand just slightly in front of the player so that you have the chance to get the ball first. Watch the flight of the ball, but be aware that your opponent may try to lose you, so watch for this, too.

Defender

Attacker

Goaltender

If you are the goaltender your positioning for a corner shot is important. If the penalty area is crowded, or you think the ball will swerve inward to the goal, stand near the center of the goal. Otherwise, stand toward the far post, with a defender between you and the post. This is the best place from which to watch the flight of the ball.

Goaltender

Holding up an opponent

1 If your teammates have been caught out of position by a surprise counterattack, you may be left with the task of protecting an undefended goal. If so, you must play for time until help arrives. Keep the attacker at bay, rather than risk an unsuccessful tackle. Guard the attacker closely and spread your body wide to block any view of the goal.

Defenders will run back as quickly as possible.

Goal line

An attacker will shoot if given the opportunity.

Spread your arms to block the attacker's view of the goal.

2 The defenders caught out of position have two priorities. They must regain position as quickly as possible and keep in touch with the players they are supposed to be guarding. It is very likely that the player with the ball will try to pass to a teammate who may have a better chance of scoring.

Keep yourself between the attacker and the goal.

The attacking team now must get past the defenders before they can shoot.

3 When your fellow defenders are back in position, they can protect the whole penalty area. This makes it very difficult for the attackers to receive the ball and get a goal-scoring opportunity. Now you can attempt a tackle.

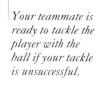

Your teammate is ready to tackle the player with the ball if your tackle is unsuccessful.

Index

Acknowledgments

Dorling Kindersley would like to thank the following people for their help in the production of this book:

Ted Hart, Eric Sommers, Malcolm Musgrove, and Mick Brealey for all their soccer help and advice; John Garrett and Matt Garrett for their patience and enthusiasm on the soccer field and in the studio; Dulwich Hamlet Football Club for the use of their ground; Colin at Soccer Scene, London, for the kits; Scott Brealey, Ben Blyth, Rene Brade, Johathan Crane, Ben Brennan, Alex Brennan, Tom Dove, Jamie Ross-Hulme, Daniel Platel,

Hannah Gardiner, Delroy Gill, Adam Habtesellasse, and Angel Watson for their skill and cooperation on the soccer field; and Djinn VonNoorden for editorial assistance.

Picture credits
Colorsport: 4*bc*, 5*br*;
Bob Thomas Sports Photography: 5*bl*, 10*tr,bl*, 11*cl,cr*, 12*tr*, 13*bl*, 15*tr,cl,br*, 17*tr*, 19*br*, 20*cl*, 22, 23*bl,br,cr*, 26*c*, 27*cr*, 30*tr*.

Additional DK photography: Andy Crawford

key: *b* bottom, *c* center, *l* left, *r* right, *t* top

Picture researcher: Lorna Ainger